Self and Simulacra

2001 BEATRICE HAWLEY AWARD

Other books by Liz Waldner

Homing Devices

A Point Is That Which Has No Part, Iowa Poetry Prize

Self

and

Simulacra

Liz Waldner

ALICE JAMES BOOKS   FARMINGTON, MAINE

ACKNOWLEDGEMENTS

Ploughshares: "Determinate Inflorescence: Ephemera"; "Off Course: Ineffable"
The Denver Quarterly: "Nor, truly, can I peremptorily deny . . ."
The Lesbian Review of Books and *Hedgebrook Journal:* "Ariadne, Her Collect and Complexion"
Conduit: "Vegetable History: Red-neck, Queer"; "Indeterminate Inflorescence: Flower Press"
Electronic Poetry Review: "Such as reduced the Heathens to Divinity . . ."; Though the radical hu-
    mour contain in it oil for seventy . . ."; "In brief, we have devoured ourselves, and do . . ."
The 'Browne' section appeared as a chapbook, *Read Only Memory*, from Seeing Eye Books.
The 'Gray' section is for Katherine: *If you think to bring pie, bring two.*
Thanks to Vermont Studio Center/Carole Maso for the fellowship and to Centrum and Villa
    Montalvo—save eight pages, this book was written on your varied and beauteous
    premises. For friendship, support, and kindness, especially while I worked on this book,
    thanks to Kamyar Arasteh, Tim Tucker, and the Accianis.

Alice James Books gratefully acknowledges support from the University of Maine at Farming-
ton and the National Endowment for the Arts.

Alice James Books are published by the Alice James Poetry Cooperative, Inc., an affiliate of the
University of Maine at Farmington.

ALICE JAMES BOOKS
238 MAIN STREET
FARMINGTON, ME 04938

www.umf.maine.edu/~ajb

Library of Congress Cataloging-in-Publication Data
Waldner, Liz.
    Self and simulacra / Liz Waldner.
        p. cm.
    ISBN 1–882295–32–3 (alk. paper)
    I. Title.

PS3573.A42158 S45   2001
811'.54—dc21   2001046235

Cover illustration: Hannah Höch, *Dompteuse* (Tamer), c.1930, photomontage, Kunsthaus
Zürich, © 2001 Artists Rights Society (ARS), New York / Bild-Kunst, Bonn.

CONTENTS

i. Gray

ii. Browne

iii. More Encounters With Remarkable Men or Other

PROLOGUE

* * *

SIMULACRUM, n; L. pl—lacra.   1. an image; something which is formed in the likeness of a being or thing.   2. a phantom; esp., a vague, unreal semblance; a mock appearance; a sham. (Webster's New International Dictionary, 1921 India Paper Edition)

What is within us surrounds us.   (Rilke)

A man's [sic] life is characteristic of himself.   (Jung)

We have found that the recurrence of identical or similar data in con-tiguous areas of space or time is a simple empirical fact which has to be accepted and which cannot be explained by coincidence . . . (Paul Kammerer)

The experiencer himself [sic] continues to exist always and every-where as the object of experience.   (Kashmir Shaivism)

It is God who, in the form of knowledge, is known through every object . . .   (Swami Muktananda)

mon semblable, mon frère . . .   (Baudelaire)

* * *

Gray

. . . in which the plants of a country—especially of our own—are described.

—Asa Gray,
*Gray's Lessons in Botany
and Vegetable Physiology*

Off Course: Ineffable

O small sunlight on the bark which faded before I could finish my
    sentence
and so changed my sentence in its course,
so change me.

My course is rotten, I channel Mr. Berryman who am not such a man.
Then let my form of address or my address withal place me
zipcode not withstanding in the right relation to
the world, the one that doesn't every second
fetch the self its mirror or
implore the self to clear
its sinuses: the plus and minuses interest only in the Fibonacci
    series—

Here I answered a wrong number, and see it is too late. Even here
(Leaves as a Contrivance for Increasing the Surface)
the laminae make up the face. Of course
the cotyledon wearies.

The Course of True Love (to *die Männer* born)

Everything was prepared, and even formed,
Beforehand. Growing in a different manner
As well as in opposite directions, they began.
Wanner later, yet yearned, strove, bestowing
(manna) Un(h)armed the simulacra of self—a bad
Turn. The divided sign, and the time making it was
All necessity would—dared—ask behind (hosanna)
That mask they claimed to know like skin: to a thin
Performance, to a wan precept, to a worn perceptorium,
Welcome. *Wilkhommen.* They grew newly from a decimal system.
Women? They blew gender, hummed 'big spender,' but what they knew
(multi-tasking) Was *battlement stormed*, was *cloudy parapet*,
And brae, not *burn*; even "lovely percept," was an agitation
Of an evening in a small room
For as long as one could see—
Was stone upon artificed stone.

Duty Again and Again Desire (finish work)

Now it is our bounden duty
in all times and in such places
to write away from the edge of the cliff
to send off such boxtops as would procure Safety
to proffer that match to wax where the wick has given up
to act as a wick, soot on the fingers become dark heart
dark way, what will—become of me were I to say
yes to her and yet another place, another is-
lander carpenter, off the coast of Maine...

My aplomb has left me and with it
the ability to build a right doorway—or
recognize, even, the off angles of desire

Indeterminate Inflorescence: Flower Press

A spadix is nothing but a fleshy spike or head
(Ament, sister, ament) Last night in this bed
you once enjoyed us in for days on end, I said
out loud the things you said to me then. I bled,
too, just as before and saw you coming through
either door of this room where there are three and you
commonly covered by a peculiar enveloping leaf, true,
had nothing new to say or do and I, nothing to be(e)/d.

Vegetable physiology. The other shovel with which I tried to bury
preserved yours—I was in a hurry and misjudged the depth,
your heft, his tiny whine and worry—yet his favor I couldn't curry
compels; I want him because I would not plant him much in me.
Nature abhors bereft. He was a woman and you were a man
and I with two in the hand surrendered each to the nearest bush.
Neither a burrower nor a surrenderer bee; when push
comes to shovel from now on, I push.

The Unmourning Water of the Writing Pen

Flower: is it a flower?
Mist: is it a mist?

One doesn't like to push one's luck
or one does, for one does. Push:
will is a fire. My skin when I begin
to draw the world
to me. With a pen.

Under lamplight your hair lay like long grass
on a pillow—   under the leafbud—
that is, polypetalous—   past ('I' begin)
the axis of the bloomed you
passing through that video viewing room.

Spring fed on winter; winter, a word
to call to me. Does a word push ever?
Ever, a long wait place. Heretofore
not enough distance to plait another's
Hereness. Yet last night, your girl hair

there—couched—my touch
when you were not aware.
Se terre, in(de)ter—
the lung of the air
silence pairs:

the tongue around the 't' in *enter*
subterranean forms of the stem—

Vernation

It is said to be inflexed or reclined in vernation
        morphology of the receptacle adoration of the tabernacle
           odalisque her thighs

It is said to be conduplicate, as in the Magnolia the Cherry the Oak
        downy upper lip, the lower two-lipped ray flower
           half-adherent sighs

It is said to be plicate
        the calyx and the corolla
           genuflect axillary, irregularity of hilar parts

If rolled it may be so from the tip downward
        crosier, tongue of butterfly

And it is said to be circinate
        sash, vegetable fabric, window sill, climbing vine

When it is rolled from both edges it is said to be convolute
        as in the Apricot

Or it may be sometimes inwards when it is involute
        as in the Violet

Or it may be sometimes outwards when it is revolute
        as in the Azalea, whose deliquescent stem—

As it was in the beginning is now and ever shall be
        ordinarily of leaves

With the spiry branches that proceed it, as of palms the hearts
        and in the Morning-Glory twisted, besides.

Bisection (cheering, vivi-)

The flowers themselves are like knees,
not their buds, as with peonies,
the ball-peened. She calls me
from too far away for not even a kiss
yet, could be like violets, too,
that end's her spectrum. Say
lustrum, hurt one. Say I do
Teena, too. See how, too, I am
on my knees. Say I too know
what *you* means.

Vegetable History: Red-neck, Queer

I grew up in a darkness of rhubarb
from it I learned to grow leaves large enough
to cover the ruinous red that supported me

rue anemone was a plant I liked as a rhubarb
its curvy girl leaves
sweet so not   for ruinous me

the sun shone down and I came up without the help
of farmers doctors relatives or much of any
thing save rain   roots I grew in my head

which is why I'm such a sad red stalk here where
they can't even look at me and get "pie"
out right   (she explained)

rain I love and always will, yet know snow is my birthright
trees are my several souls and dirt the birds of those souls
and lady bugs console rueful me who

(was) moved   (rhubarb can't, except to die forsooth
                            forsake the earth, etc.—)
really it was being tapped lightly with a stalk
a ribbony sheen of rhubarb stalk, she, its arc

touched me and I came up upright again (resurrect)
to light   that
was me

Determinate Inflorescence: Ephemera

I am not making myself up for public consumption.
I enjoy consumption when it means an end to things.

Please deduce.
                              Each flower comes from the axil
of a small leaf which, however, is often so small
that it might escape notice and which sometimes
(as in the Mustard Family) disappears altogether.
(*Waving adieu, adieu, adieu.*) The summit, never
being stopped by a terminal flower may go on to grow
and often does so, producing lateral flowers
one after another, the whole summer long.

                                                          Ok.

My raceme to your umbel. You terminal,
me currant, choke-cherry, barberry. You milk
weed, you flat cyme to my corymb, my kiss alas
like a moth on the right flower at the wrong time of day.

Cleave vs. Cleave, occasion for a little play

for Diana

She said something about me to me,
You negotiate silence, which because I don't know
what it means could be true. There is room for the truth
in ignorance; what I know is nothing
like what I know
(___)is true. I felt
naked hearing something and I felt naked
was so dangerous it is true there was
little room for anyone beside fact that naked
(so, and, but) I left the little room.

Marginalia:

Chapter One: Who gives a fig, in which... (see, sycophant?)

Synopsis: *Leaf* would have been a simple thing to say

(Earlier That Same Day:) Perfect Cleavage—"a diamond is not a metal,"
I informed her, a form of being proud of guessing "tungsten"

Shame: to be visible

A Shame: to pass unseen

Is This How to Conduct a Life?

The match makes a fine wick
3 candles and a Cinderella slipper
made of mandarin peels

Last night I ate the one
offered as an incense holder; bolder
now, I interfere with fire

"Intervene" sounds missionary
"interfere" merely mean

yet when you don't know how
anyone will take what you mean
and you don't have an outcome in mind

beyond *meet me in this moment,*
let me see and be seen, interfere
is braver or interfere is

what happened to the Santa Clara valley here
so the only apricot trees are museum pieces
and the smog and killed things also

All a non sequitur
says a sequoia
Allah— Selah—

The night simile, 'right,' I mean—
the asking *let me*
that's the clue to me—

Unwind me. My cue: "could be."
Trees burn.
Encouraged, I cotyledon on.

Poor Cotyledon

A Bean affords a similar and more familiar illustration:
The proper material is nourishing matter. Neither water
nor scotch nor solitude which the plantlet yet imbibes
from generous earth will answer the purpose. (Some moth

never harkens, battens, eats a new thing, only feeding ever
on the caterpillar it once was.) Nor answers elaborate solitaire
to harsh nourish in its two green leaves. In the ordinary
sore way hankers—a canker—after connection; vegetal tissue
that night climbed mortar to flicker—night breeze—a border for
lamp-lit scene: within, mortal convene, venial advent; lip-bit
reflection without: Congenial Dinner Party Through A Window Seen—
whilst seated at same table.

Unable to succeed in becoming leaflike
never to display the real nature of leaves—

the proper material, 'f'-able—O People!
its sweet and eatable seed

On First Looking Into Gray's *Botany*

Last Supper First

> *Then, Love said. you must taste my meat*
> *So I did sit and eat.*
>
> (George Herbert, "Love (III)")

i.

Veritable physiology
vert mange, blanc mange
very *cha(i)r*itable
vegetable physiology

(forfending)

ii.

to which is added a copious
GLOSSARY
or Buffet of Botanical Terms

(attending)

iii.

inorganic: unorganized: no organs

their parts do not answer to one another

not note and note, a bird

nor mist and mist, a flower

they were formed but they did not grow

nor did they proceed from previous bodies like themselves

nor have they the power of producing another similar body

nor do I sing

for one

of my parts does not answer
did it never answer?
another—oh how is
answer like another?

an die musik
a taking in

a fit, a tailor, a consumptive
composer, decomposer, *echt*-diner

look   the past does not hurt me
see   similar words on a page

(rending)

I'm a Bit Transformed (chalk-full)

behold the inorganic world, or mineral kingdom

where do you live?
mineral kingdom

what is your name?
mineral kingdom

who made you?
mineral kingdom

destitute of life, said Asa Gray.

The First of Time

Ripen, fall, and cease . . .

At first,
small and imperfect,
it grows and develops
by powers of its own

and so I love it

       (I know not but it may be of moment
       for those who come after

for each individual owes its existence
to a preceding one   like itself

under the influence of life

                     life departs

       (to hazard the loss indeed of all I had

the giant's house is empty so

                     a little while

in the story life   life then begins again

she can have a baby

being-able-to-have a condition
can's every Thing

life deposits

                                                  5 cents decomposes

into earth and air again

why do we get to live?

what likeness
          does the cow bear   to the grass
it feeds upon?

grass is not without will
being eaten is not evidence
time not a function   of reasons

study the way
a living being lives

how this is done it is the province of
Vegetable Physiology to explain

still,
        an explanation is
                                only a likeness
only like another Thing.

In So Dismal a Calamity

Style is being yourself but on purpose. (Quentin Crisp)

so briskly locomotive
as her hair

leaves, &c.
blossoms, &c.

limbs or members
at all resemble

reassemble place
place possess

nourish as its wants
take as one's own

oh, enough
for all to eat

why should one
not an other?

just
so

Style II

the simplest & most persistent
is *what for?*

its ramifications, growth—
I have neither roots nor branches

yet I am able
to bear *still yet, despite*

all these years
the trees say *daughter*

however (I say) there
is no Where I belong

and none to whom.

Should I be alive?
Must I?

       persist

the study of the way
       a living being lives,
       and grows, and performs
       its various operations

because it gives
       that kind of knowledge
       which it is desirable
       each should possess

fulfill the purposes of their existence

give rise

in their fossil remains

     to fruit

How, Now

the problem of sex to solve
she set herself

a candle at each elbow
burned

at 40, at 8:40, arrived
in August so alive

and by November nigh
entombed in the crust of the earth

a town of 3200, few sidewalks
many churches marriages

despair, sit in a chair
Cheez-it, my old friend, would that you instead

devoured me   burned only
by memory   I couldn't see

(smoke, eyes) an answer
still, I tried

What Is True in a General Way

I lifted the candle to drink.
The heater ever on, my head shorn—

January, February
this plantlet formed in the seed

the embryo a little ear within
which gives to Spring its greatest charm

the rigors of our long winter
the hands of leaf unfold

Such touch to be desired
calling

given that longing does not change
to prove with a sigh the candle flame

Here's green tea the same
a dozen years only

my brain's changed—it doesn't want any
more to know

At length they blossom
bear fruit and produce
seeds like those from which they grew.

Shall we commence with the seedling
just rising from the ground?

Oh dear.

Nor Any Other "Instrument Submerged"

than sharp a knife
nor microscope
nor wordable witness

does *here*
it hurts mean cut
more or not?

even the dullest beholder
can then hardly fail to ask

what does she live upon?
what her object and use?

A: Of Vegetation in General

When it had merely to unfold and grow
        its little stem named the Radicule
        by mistake were better named the Caulicle
        but it is not expedient to change
old names

later, a third pair of leaves
grew my name, tree speech

embryo like a little ear, hear
I write you call me

B: *Catalogue Raisoné*

The tree in itself in its whole vegetation
has nothing more in kind
(the Thing in itself
no more in mind)

The embryo an epitome
repeating itself upwardly
of the herb or tree to be—
deduce, induce, conduce, adduce?

Thus was I born too deeply
buried? or am not yet?

In mind
bore seed
of kind
and rind

Rabe:

the organs of vegetation are tired

      (malathion, Round Up, ADM's friends
           yet with light and air
   dioxin, pcb, ozone, et alia.
           the opposite growth of root and stem begin

           at the beginning of germination
           one ever seeking to bury
           itself the other striving
           toward sun and air

           how the plantlet makes these movements
           we cannot explain nor how it knows
           which way to go)
   and we do not know or

care.

Browne

GOD being all things is contrary unto nothing . . .

—Sir Thomas Browne

Such as reduced the Heathens to Divinity . . .

In our study of Anatomy there is
A mass of mysterious Philosophy,
Kyrie sounds and loud fornicating
Sounds and sounds of I am become
Stupid, my heart through a sieve
Conceived the need to birth you
(*As night conceives the sea sounds in silence*)
But beach heads breach instead so I
Conceive myself the miserablest
Person extant. Sextant; *leaves*
Fall inside the bishop's skull
And all; why withal are ways all
Lost amongst strait ligaments?
And stars and dawn? Mere emoluments;
I walk on, administering my Self
In the face (ow) of fresher freshet:
Waters broke, I dote on hope yet
Once I spoke could never measure
Out your Fabrick. Days later smoking
("All fire signs, how painful," opined
The astrologer at the dinner table)
With the cook who always felt my meat,
He quotes you: "He lost me when *she*
Fucks a carp." (He little knew me.)
Lightning, thunder, smolder, smoke—
So the Fabrick's patterned, bolt by bolt,

My share canopic only. I am (scarp,
Scree) fallen, Egypt, fallen. See?
The leaf-mould out the arterial earthworm
Now leaf-vein of the kale I steam
On a hot-plate in my room, soon
(Among green mountains and their green
Removing vales, anodyde)
More remotely in myself carnified.

Thus I am and know not how; I fall
And fear falling as I fall. Call it implicit
Sense: *all flesh is grass* not only
Metaphoric; cadaverous Reliquaries
Walk content beneath the trees
Called I's and thee's and, crudely, he's and she's;
You gone, I grieve the first EVEning
Walking through unquiet absence to
Where yellowed grass in a square means Where
And moss where were our hearts.
Well. I believe the letters sent you
Are digested into flesh-you; the next fish
Your nipple bit tasted mine, too.
Troll, rill—until—not anything
Of moment more: there is
Something in us that can be
Without us, and Will.

I must confess a great deal of obscurity . . .

Nor any light though I dwelt in the body of the Sun
Nor manifest a Scale of creatures; rising not disorderly
(My extremest circumstance: over-writ within your Vale,
Ascribe the accidents and properties of the Many to the One)
Upon the first motion of my reason, your angels
Tutelary, Guardian, their comely wings bestir.
A resistless weight is everywhere—so my reason
Is the better part of nothing. Light invisible? Give me,
Rather, shadow's green . . . *Seen.*   Do I comprehend
Your nature? No; it is the method of the Schools.
Yet I am sure there is a common spirit at play within
Us its *instrument submerged.* Retain the fir—the first
Of Porphyry for yourself: say your name into this day.
Yet I saw it by your halt hand made—on a paper in a Bank.
My breath banked beside you fore-ran the ruine
Of an outcast state. (Here reason reasons *Not Again*)
Celestial Coal—outside, this heat. And inside—
Must I a creature be—her? Existence so mere
She cannot speak? Help me. Hear: "When thou first
Camest thou strokedst me, wouldst give me
water with berries in't and teach me how to name
the bigger light and how the less that burn by day
and night: and—" Though there be but one to sense
There are two to reason and Reason likes it not:
Nor any light, nor Mr. Man, his mind his own;
I one poor amphibious piece of hope: Ms. Caliban.

Nor, truly, can I peremptorily deny . . .

My wanting wanted without study or deliberation to know things
By their forms. The specifical difference between your hand compatible
And your mind not: as beyond the extremest circumference. [He created
No new World; she actually existing is but hopes and probability;
She are, in one nature, those five kinds of existences, those names
Of things he can't think, the mystical method of Moses bred up,
Fed and watered into Bloom: 1) the *Magisterial record of breath*
And breath 2) *the breath conveying* which so moves the body
It informs 3) *the ubiquitary breath* which, while subsisting all alone
Is yet middle, happy, and participatory 4) *the breath styled a bare*
Accident which is most the similitude of GOD 5) *breath conformant.*]

To call ourselves a Microcosm, or little World—in a tent, yet—
I thought it only a pleasant trope of Rhetorick, a trick of intense
Instance, the Particular become our own upon restraint of time
Restraint of place, and denial of distance. I thought all wrong.

Pardon. A determinate mansion planted beside a copse whence
Rained the night long the Really All Things of fir-y cotyledon—

Pardon.   It was that work involved in finding my skin
That made me microcosm him. Each are that great and true

Amphibium, the one dividing and distinguishing the two
Worlds Will would have made one:

                                        what before GOD I wanted
Him to be and what before me, wonted, he was.

An impression and tincture of reason . . .

She played the sensible operator but a little While.
GOD being all things is contrary unto nothing; why not I?
So she smote herself. So she set herself to win Omnity
From Nullity in her sublunary estate-and-sleeping bag.
Honor in the honorer rather than the honored; now await
Ministring Spirits to deliver venery's de- and re-ceipt: To make
A man without conjunction pick a number, Crasis and Temper:
Long wait. Another simple, another scruple, little slumber;
A harder substance like her—self—symmetry and proper
Disposition of the Organs picked not from leaves of any author
But bred amongst the tares and many weeds of her
Own brain. In vain. As weakly that the World was dear,
External, adjunct, even homage (honor proved external
Too) to her Cause, so at the blast of his mouth were her Creatures
All unmade. At his bare word the raised walls of his cells came
Tumbling down in cymes and umbels. (Separated materials,
Lives at a distance even in himself.) Everywhere where is
The flat form affirmative of Plato, she'd raise now a little mound
Audient, austral: genitive, genital: auscultative auricle:
Miniscule wave aroused within the inner sea so
Disputing in the auditory Germane . . . If only she
Had in his or he in hers—cusp and couloir—whisper'd the Ear.

Get thee to a summary . . .

For as they proceed, they but ever multiply
His name and shadow in the earth. I need not envy

The temper of Daws and Crows a-strut upon
A cemetery lawn; green in black feather shows

Multiples in green.
                By the privilege, departed soul
Of my departed nature, I perish quaternary.

Grave-maker, with my toes   those
Narrow obligations to the world, I set aside

Such umbrage of the four unquiet quarters
By making shadow greater, or pretend to

Celestine . . .
                The shallow hopes your hipbones mark
My terraces would see(m). *I know all the best holes.*

You said it yet you won't dig me. I dig them
Feelingly. My own into my own loam (my home

Away from Home), that soiled soul and dormitory
Of mischief, blood & allegory, unbeseeming

As it seems.
                Cable, Cable, why'd you leave me?
John Cale moans for me. I run on here like Mercury

(One touch has rolled and bowled me) but to be
Retrograde hereafter: what on earth is wrong

With me? I need another song; I wake my taking
Slow, like so: the fruitful indecision of the uncial

Is where I'd be;
                  is where, you departed, my feet
Lead me; letters in tow, grave processional,

Earthmould and Vespillo, incense my pillow.
'Darkness,' darkness sings. Swale; s(w)ing low.

I pray for 'Unbeknownst' like dawn
Breaking in a second story, a fecund second

Story Man to be,
              by dint of Open and of Free
(Coulisse, coulotte, and cotter pin undone larkily)

Able to plant the plot in me, majuscule: Everything
Under the skin is deep and the skin is also deep. O,

Someone be the one for me.
                  It is not suspect, fun, no.
It's all the fault of the fourth of July and one Fool

Rotten Father: Fault his flag improperly gotten. Nor
Is tent's flap nor lip's detente no grave-marker. Now

You must excuse me, departed soul, for I really must be
                        g(r)o(w)ing.
(Hooray for Captain Spaulding, Master of Vexillology.)

Though the radical humour contain in it oil for seventy . . .

I can but plea, it seems; how this goes hard upon me—
Green (the skin of the earth) sward—one word—
I would feel and make you feel. Can no woman
Live well once but she that could live twice?
Splice me—so am I a Child. May I twice be
And thus worthy of her knees. For I am upon them
In my heart where I am scabbed (and superannuate)
From wanting in. In wanting in is how she prays
Some more. (and annotates.) (and waits.)
                                    In my warm blood and Canicular
Days—How can you not kiss me? I have but forty
Seconds used; twenty to my lips remain since an auricular
Circumspection sold me short—my compunction
Cut me—short—

Here the grass a paler green beneath is where I lay beside you
Where the trees' eyes wept the little sounds I heard inside you
Now the knees erase the trace of these with skin to be denied you
Address, redress, dress me up and down and in "We all therein
Become but Pantalones to my severer contemplation . . ."

Reductio . . .

Call: He strives to go the neatest way unto corruption

Response: sound of cycad friction. Sound of bad disposition
Turned worse habit. Garment never rent but rather gentle
Delved under: desire does not rectify but render rather
Incurvate my spine. There is not long enough a line
To contain its Anticks asymptotic. (twelvemo
And twelve tone row and mop-and-mow
Responsory for such lectio
As opinion; license
At a distance...

Call: He seeks in any rete the suppos'd repose of death
Response: restiveness

In brief, we have devoured ourselves, and do . . .

As they leave Earth—here I falter—stealing
Into our hearts to be a kind of nothing
            (The exactest element for us)
Yet tremble nonetheless
At the name of Death—as they leave earth
Is the absence of Organ or Instrument
Amongst all those curious pieces (Clavicle.
Psalter.) in the body of each loved being
For Soul to be a comfort and redeem? I cannot more
Darken my speech. That a beast doth perish
Entreats a moment's breath from me
Merely knowing not where'd it go,
How can this be? So the possibility
Of you, gone—so should have gone—
From me. No further verity. I have been
Materialled into Life, I have sat beside you
Beside myself with watching your mouth
As you speak, I have loved the words
Of your mouth so that my perishing will be
Unlike a beast's—yet without
Testimony other than my pen's.
Dismal conquest in digestion.
If all I am came in at my mouth
What then is SING? Some of I am
Came in at yours or yours came being into me
When I heard—I grazed—*a gamma flower*
Opening quotidian
                The news how I would die:
You dreamed the dream I gave you
But woke beside some other I.

Wherein our bones with stars shall make one Pyre . . .

There is no item of your coming.
I am sad long hope is at an end. I hate the end.
My special hatred of Death cannot such patient Sad forfend.

Had you returned even one hour early
The statute-madness of the World had died daily.
That there may be more world than my Soldier hope has hoped—

Horae combustae only. *Felix esse mori?*
It is a lesson to be good. I tried—try—am tried.
My wanting unabated though the insolent part of reason lied—

So the perfectest actions of earth console me
Not. Nor can such saying allay an aching punctual.
I ought perpend: the beautiful path through the stone of water...

Can the sunfish drown?
Again shall the Vessel say to the Potter
Why hast thou made me thus? Let me rather
(or more of the same) Be in love with dead Sir Thomas Browne.

More Encounters with Remarkable Men or Other

Dear Sir,
I am in a madhouse & quite forget your Name or who you are
You must excuse me for I have nothing to communicate or tell of
& why I am shut up I dont know I have nothing to say so I
conclude

Yours respectfully
John Clare

A Genitive Case *(Desiderus)*

I wish there were a photograph of my hands when they were younger.
     I can't remember.

My fingers look like people, now in baggy clothes, the kind I favor.
     Is this causal?

"Micro-Lamarckian" could be my tribe, my life's title,
     an address label:

Observe the object of desire become desire
     for a star.

Call the Question

je seme à tout vent

i.

How can I expect or be expected to keep up with my sins
so to confess them each and all and not die with one on my soul?

How come there used to be St. Francis
would bring you back to life so you could confess
and die in the Lord, to the confusion of the devil?

How can I (ashamed of Rwanda, Bopal, death row, NAFTA, SUV)
live in the new polis which is the clamor of tv
when it offers me citizen-immunity: the dose of the drug
(shameful viewing of others' shame) increased daily?

How come nobody seems to notice there's nobody there to see?

ii.

The desire to brag is desire for desire.

More important is to have a witness.
The writer writes therefore.

(*Therefore*)
In the mirror more and more

I look like what I am.
To appear is my every desire.
You are a boat for my desire.

Do you float or does somebody ride you?

iii.

She asks herself.
The disruption of writing instead
'asked' herself almost
undid me. Let us have none of the implications
of the past in our future. Please. Suh.

Mississippi, *mon lecteur.*
"Mon lecteur" is everything. Therefore
compare to the era of "See Emily Play," or
rather compare it to nothing for nothing compares:
in it, "I" was a live.

iv.

What is the thing I call mine in me?
Has it aught to do with you, *mon Bien*, who
are a girl like a rill and blonde to boot?

It ought.

v.

for honey I call
for honey I call

vi.   (-aphore)

for it turns off Panopticon's camera
for: it keeps "thou" in the picture, for

it keeps the seer's boat afloat—
the *seme* in seem's sole hope?

DAMASCENE. Sin tax, *impuesto,* put it there, swell.

Without taxis, we go nowhere.
Like a horse was for us, before us:
we feed them money and ride.
We tell them where we want to go
but with our mouths, instead of theirs.

The words of our mouths, they are taxing.
Each day a new percentage is paid
to raising Cain and capital—letters
—of credit and credence—accrue,
mortgaging meaning against which to borrow
or, better, construe
syntax, that ride in the cab
from an 'I' to a 'thou'
on a map made of need for a map.

Nuestro plano, pater noster,
up around us pile the scales
with which we measure 'daily'
and despair. Give unto us
the return fare. An insider's tip
would lift us up and put your money
on (and in) our hearts—those han(d)som(e) cabs
whose veils of dust we invest with sense
out of hope for a fair return.
Deliver from us those we thus make to travail.
Lead me, let me (leaded fuel) arrive at you.
"Pen," "pain," and "pant" in hand,
without bridle or bit (groom nor wound),
put me beside you. Read this want
as daily b*read*, cast upon still waters.

Say what (so far with my days) I've said:
syntaxis means to stay and requires
both its hire and its 'here';
in this way stone is turned to loaves
and miles of Where returned to Here.
(If thou asketh for the bread of Here
will he give thee the stone of Where?
No.)

So.
In this light (Damascene) taste and see
how much I want to ride your grammar,
how good it costs to hire my car.

Ariadne, Her Collect and Complexion

—at Double Bluff Beach

The voice said, Kneel down.
I knelt.

The voice said, Ask the question.
Where to go? (I asked) How to know?

Before me, entire erstwhile trees
become driftwood, a bleached nest
unwound as a skein, pleached at the foot
of a cliff of clay occasionally raining
itself down in waterfall of clod and dust—

There were, I heard, footsteps behind me
and turning to look saw the Sound,

wave upon wave
arrive, arrive

and the long blue bluffs
of all the other shores
complecting them here.

Buoyancy, gravity, and of what
we are made: *the Cause that*
will not show itself but indicates:

more in the verb
than in the noun

more in the kneeling
than in the fear of going,
unknowing, down

Routine Fidelities

In the night
I walk around the empty house
singing "We Are Climbing Jacob's Ladder."
It's cold, it's June on the Strait of Juan de Fuca.
I open the door to breathe the air.
I open the air. Frogs sing there.

In the evening
the water at the foot of the cliff
made a noise in my head
meaning: I could fall
meaning: I could be falling.
It was part of the view.
I could see it.

It is silent except for my pen in here.
There is a man on a farm in a there
who is bothered by how alone I am
again and again in all my wheres.
He contemplates.
He prays to Jesus.
I imagine I hear part of his prayer
considering how he wanted to touch me here.

Here, others are more usually
bothered by the weather.

I look in the mirror so I am there.
I sing so I make a noise.

I would be joyful.
I would say my prayer

(here I wait)

It appears unless I'm singing
we are climbing Jacob's ladder
nothing's doing here.

A Letter Heaven-*Sent*

The cloud lays the ladder
of its word upon the water.
Unlike its word, the cloud is still.
Unlike its word, the cloud is clear.

Who can read its word? The body of water
renders it cursive: deduce a hand
deduce intent, as ever, leap
to "for me?" This, evidence.

Evidence of things unseen: faith.
What is seen in things unseen?
The almost seen? Yearn is
Not the same as reason.

Let us reason together, saith the Word.
If I touch my face to the face of the water—
do I cease to be if here I breathe?

In a dark window bright people
walk hand in hand at an angle
up into sky.

Is it wrong to dream this dream of With?
Is it hope for a place in the sentence "I"
Laid down by cloud on water?

My doom: What (I) want
Is to be addressed.
What I want is to be meant.

Last Friday, 7 PM

Sort of like a jar in Tennessee I sat on a bench
where *jar* is not poetic bird, at least
I tried to have some
sort of human life which I had taken
to include human contact at least
of word into ear   an empty jar where
an invisible vowel, cobweb, part of some
bug that didn't need it anymore
didn't spell anything and nothing
drew near

The Question of the Red Sulfur

It is not Martin Luther
To the door his 95 articles
Hammering.

It is not Martina Navratilova,
Oriflamme,
Her matches.

It is not the muscled upper
Arm or is it. Or is it
Thew and sinew of the inner

Thigh where touched
The angel, sigh, her thumb.
Sigh, sigh. Thump. Put

The question of
The red sulfur
Before god.

Use all what
Your living body
You can find

To ask her.
Pray her to answer
And

Uniquely as your flesh has heard—
              What eyes have not
              Nor any ears
              Nor east, nor west
              The hairs of her breast
                        (numbered, count)
              Have heard—
She answers, in a word.

In the Penumbra of the Portrait of
W. A. Mozart, à Peruke

There is no greater pleasure than pleasure in writing
for even sex is its constant possibility
and even food but who (wanting
sex) cares?

Witness: I got lost in the course of my sentence
it is true, oh, but never a sin yet sudden I felt
the loss of that

(goddam this right margin)

pleasure
(collision with powdery wi(n)gs)

Oh, O, for some other collusion collision
god yes I'd bed him in his movie too—
however, I'm telling you. Like him,
some neither/nor girl.

Can you feel me telling you? I am, I do—

You, too, your you I've never known
reading these words I'm telling for you
right with you skin
here touched there for how
else knew how I would feel and I do
touching you?

Use Makes Master (an Ablative of Means)

i.
for you are the only poet

ii.
for to suffer is to become like

iii.
for the desire to become like
       is the object of one's desire to know

iv.
for the sufferer makes a place
       in the body in which to welcome the desired

v.
for in this way is a ( ) known

vi.
for in this place is welcome given/form

vii.
for your pleasure is motion to
       respond to imagined

viii.
for there's only the one bone
       but it is broken every minute

ix.
for the inability to explain
       the nature of that pleasure

x.

for you never meant *benison*

xi.

for how the sentence's backs are broken
        as the banks of rivers are broken

xii.

for it is false power, the holding
        of the other's fear in your own hands

xiii.

for on a park bench, a man said to his watch
        "you sexy thing": an I heard in wonder

xiv.

for after writing *flower* (you understood)
        write: *is it a flower?*

xv.

for *(and how often have I not observed)* the imitation
        begets the reality

xvi.

for "thou look'st like the antichrist in that lewd hat"

xvii.

although *even the rain washes its hands of me*
        will never be your middle name.

Tyler

Is it true you have the instincts of a small bird?
And thus no need of research methods?
What else do you not need?
I am so pleased

your feathers
wing me
here

Adjure Injure: Last Call

After a while the white night clouds climbed up
over the ragged edges of red-wooded ridges and came
toward the moon, and came toward the valley. Serried,
singular and slow, ribbed the moonlit sky and with the moon's light
conjured a pond ring of pink, a pattern of stay like the ocean's
in despite of its waves' constant motion, in their sailing through of sky.

To the east and beneath, the hundred year yews
and the eucalyptus bore between their blackened blues
a solitary bar, luminous, lenticular—and as I
looked I saw and saw I was able to see. Everything I want
is to be in love with the world like this, as I used to be,
to feel this seeing I now call being
and knew as the dark heart of 'me.'

Paul Kammerer devoted much of his life to proving Lamarck's theory that an organism may be affected by its environment and pass the adaptations so effected to its offspring. His acute observation of the imaginary borderland between organism and its environment included a life-long study of what Jung, reading Kammerer's voluminous and charming schema/catalogue of 'serial events', later named synchronicity. A sense of the political, cultural, sexual, and scientific intrigues surrounding the struggle to discredit Lamarck (and Kammerer, who was already in big trouble for having trained as a musician), as well as an excerpt from Kammerer's work on his law of seriality, may be found in Arthur Koestler's book, *The Case of the Mid-Wife Toad.* Darwin and Lamarck's differences are slight but their valency great; that arriving at fact, interpreting data and interrogating theory are, inescapably, matters of projecting, deflecting, and/or embracing a worldview, which is to say casting and dodging one's likeness and shadow, is apparent in the story of Darwin's ascendancy, and in the history of the uses to which their disagreements (and ramifications thereof) have been put. Because we are not separate from our 'environment', the conjuring of fact from 'what is within us' looks like the conjuring of a self, as does the essaying/assaying of meaning from these. These are social labors requiring social support and leisure; instead, we are directed to become isolate, profit-generating consumers, especially of others' meanings. How then must we live? > who is we? > what is a self?

Section 1: Gray

The Course of True Love: "lovely percept" is from "A Chance Which Does Redeem" in *Homing Devices* (O Books, 1998); *die Männer:* German; the men.

Determinate Inflorescence: Ephemera: "Waving Adieu, Adieu, Adieu" is a Wallace Stevens poem.

67

Cleave vs. Cleave: "perfect cleavage" in the geological sense, as well.

Last Supper First: Fr., *chair*—flesh.

The First of Time: from *The Giant's House*, by Elizabeth McCracken.

Nor Any Other "Instrument Submerged": "here it hurts," from Dürer's self-portrait in which he points to his heart; see also "I am a woman in the shape of an instrument . . . " in Adrienne Rich's "Planetarium."

Catalogue Raisoné: Kant's *Dinge an Sich,* "thing in itself," composted.

Section 2: Browne

General timbre and particular locutions from saturations in Sir Thomas Browne's works. Scattered italicizations from the poetry of Wallace Stevens and Cort Day.

I must confess a great deal of obscurity . . . : "When thou first camest thou strokedst me . . . " from Caliban's speech in *The Tempest.*

Get thee to a summary . . . : "Hooray for Captain Spaulding, the African explorer . . . " and Groucho's response: " . . . I really must be going," as sung in a Marx Brothers movie.

Section 3: More Encounters With Remarkable Men Or Other
(an amendment of the Gurdjieff title)

A Genitive Case: in which Lamarckian grammar recapitulates ontology. In my version of ancient Greek, the object of a verb designating desire is put in the genitive rather than accusative case, as the source of one's coming-to-be.

Call the Question: "*je seme à tout vent*" is the Libraire Larousse motto, usually accompanied by the image of a woman blowing the fluff from a dandelion: "I sow/seed with every wind/breath. See Arendt's discusion of *o dokei moi* (the Socratic "it seems to me") in *The Life of the Mind*. "*mon lecteur*" is Baudelaire's; "See Emily Play" is the Pink Floyd version; "Panopticon" is Foucault's.

Ariadne, Her Collect and Complexion: "complect'—to plait together; to interweave; obs.: to embrace. "the Cause that will not show itself but indicates": from Brooks Hansen's wonderful novel, *The Chess Garden*, q.v. for an account of the ascendancy of the allopathic habit of mind.

Routine Fidelities: "Jacob's Ladder," Christian hymn.

DAMASCENE: of the Syrian city, famous for its silks and steel, whither St. Paul when spectacularly converted. *Impuesto*: tax. *Nuestro plano, pater noster*: Sp. and Lat., our map, our father.

Recent Titles from Alice James Books

ALICE JAMES BOOKS has been publishing exclusively poetry since 1973. One of the few presses in the country that is run collectively, the cooperative selects manuscripts for publication through both regional and national annual competitions. New authors become active members of the cooperative, participating in the editorial decisions of the press. The press, which places an emphasis on publishing women poets, was named for Alice James, sister of William and Henry, whose gift for writing was ignored and whose fine journal did not appear in print until after her death.

TYPESET AND DESIGNED BY MIKE BURTON

PRINTING BY THOMSON-SHORE